Creative MOMENTS OF Grace

An Interactive Journaling Experience

GAYLA IRWIN

BETHANYHOUSE
a division of Baker Publishing Group
Minneapolis, Minnesota

© 2017 by Gayla Irwin

Published by Bethany House Publishers
11400 Hampshire Avenue South
Bloomington, Minnesota 55438
www.bethanyhouse.com

Bethany House Publishers is a division of
Baker Publishing Group, Grand Rapids, Michigan

Printed in China

ISBN 978-0-7642-1979-5

Unless otherwise credited, Scripture quotations are from the Holy Bible, New International Version®. NIV®. Copyright © 1973, 1978, 1984, 2011 by Biblica, Inc.™ Used by permission of Zondervan. All rights reserved worldwide. www.zondervan.com

Scripture quotations marked ESV are from The Holy Bible, English Standard Version® (ESV®), copyright © 2001 by Crossway, a publishing ministry of Good News Publishers. Used by permission. All rights reserved. ESV Text Edition: 2007

Scripture quotations marked MEV are from the Modern English Version. Copyright © 2014 by Military Bible Association. Used by permission. All rights reserved.

Scripture quotations marked MSG are from The Message by Eugene H. Peterson, copyright © 1993, 1994, 1995, 2000, 2001, 2002. Used by permission of NavPress Publishing Group. All rights reserved.

Scripture quotations marked NLT are from the Holy Bible, New Living Translation, copyright © 1996, 2004, 2007 by Tyndale House Foundation. Used by permission of Tyndale House Publishers, Inc., Carol Stream, Illinois 60188. All rights reserved.

Scripture quotations marked NRSV are from the New Revised Standard Version of the Bible, copyright © 1989, by the Division of Christian Education of the National Council of the Churches of Christ in the United States of America. Used by permission. All rights reserved.

Scripture quotations marked TLB are from The Living Bible, copyright © 1971. Used by permission of Tyndale House Publishers, Inc., Wheaton, Illinois 60189. All rights reserved.

Quotation, page 4: Jeanne Guyon, Experiencing the Depths of Jesus Christ, ed. Gene Edwards, (Sargent, GA: SeedSowers Christian Books Publishing House, 1975), 8.

Quotation, page 23: George Matheson, Moments on the Mount: A Series of Devotional Meditations (New York: A.C. Armstrong, 1901), 61.

Quotation, page 73: Lewis B. Smedes, "Forgiveness—The Power to Change the Past," Christianity Today, December 2002.

Cover design by Daniel Pitts

Author is represented by Wolgemuth and Associates

17   18   19   20   21   22   23   7   6   5   4   3   2   1

Introduction

How sweet are your words to my taste,
sweeter than honey to my mouth!
Through your precepts I get understanding;
therefore I hate every false way.
Your word is a lamp to my feet
and a light to my path.

—Psalm 119:103–105 NRSV

Some of my best memories from childhood involve drawing and creating. My dad would bring home giant stacks of used paper from his office and my little brothers and I would fill the blank side with wonderful drawings of whatever captured our imaginations at that time . . . fantastic creatures, kings, queens and castles, colorful animals, or Star Wars characters. I was almost always creating something.

Then I became a grown-up and life felt busy. It didn't seem like I had room to pursue art regularly. Although I dreamed of making it a consistent part of my life, art seemed like a luxury for which I had no time.

The healing gift of creativity became tangible in my life after the traumatic death of my dear dad. During this season of grief, I signed up for an art class through a city program. Once a week, I would drive across town to my class and pour myself into the project for the day. As I would immerse myself in art, I recognized that God was using those small acts of creation to bring healing to my wounded soul.

After experiencing art's therapeutic aspect in my own life, I offered up a little prayer, asking God for ideas that bring together my love of creativity with my faith. Intrigued with the idea of keeping an art journal, I experimented with slowly writing out passages of Scripture and prayers. Then I would sit with those words for a while and see what stirred in my heart, following up with simple artistic design. I soon realized that this small practice was helping move these thoughts and words from my head to my heart.

I've come to appreciate that just about anything I do to slow down my reading, making space to ponder what God might be saying, helps me to be more receptive and ready to hear from Him. In 1685, a French woman named Madame Jeanne Guyon published a devotional book called *Experiencing the Depths of Jesus Christ*. She writes,

> If you read quickly, it will benefit you little. You will be like a bee that merely skims the surface of a flower. Instead, in this new way of reading with prayer, you must become as the bee who penetrates into the depths of the flower. You plunge deeply within to remove its deepest nectar.

I love the image of the bee that dives deeply into the depths of a flower. I want to be like that bee, plunging into the "deepest nectar" of a passage from the Bible, reflecting on who God is and what He is saying to me. In this practice of meditating on Scripture, I give God space and blessing to move deeply into my mind and heart.

I've collected some of these ideas and put them together in this art journal. On these pages you will find some different ideas to try, including ways to meditate on themes and passages from the Bible, as well as creative ways to pray. I hope you will feel freedom in how you use this book. If you'd like, go through it in order, page by page. Or flip through the pages, stopping on an idea that grabs your imagination or connects with your heart.

Sometimes, you might want a specific topic or idea. Although many of these pages match a variety of themes, here are a few suggestions . . .

- **Thankfulness:** pages 16, 18, 40, 54, 58, 66, 68
- **Struggle:** pages 6, 22, 32, 46, 48, 62
- **Promises:** pages 8, 24, 56
- **Love:** pages 10, 12, 20, 64
- **Prayers for others:** pages 26, 34, 42, 44, 52
- **Prayers for yourself:** pages 14, 28, 30, 36, 38, 50, 60, 70, 72, 74

You can use this book on your own or with a group. My prayer is that you will have fun and enjoy the company of Jesus in new ways—and draw closer to Him in the process.

Gratefully yours,

Gayla Irwin

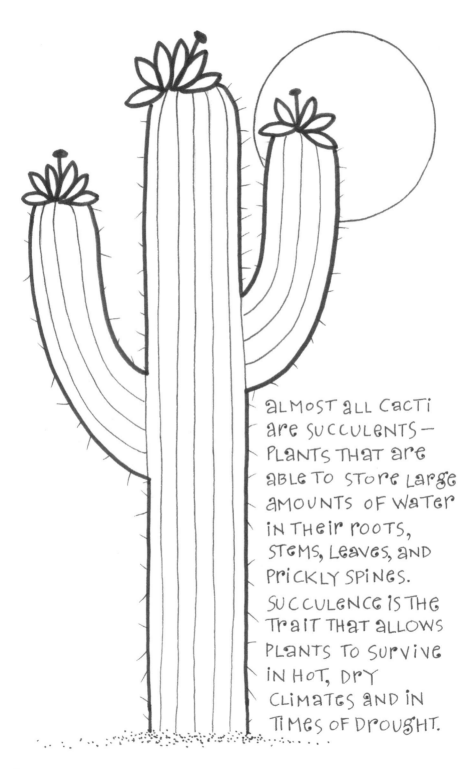

ALMOST ALL CACTI
ARE SUCCULENTS—
PLANTS THAT ARE
ABLE TO STORE LARGE
AMOUNTS OF WATER
IN THEIR ROOTS,
STEMS, LEAVES, AND
PRICKLY SPINES.
SUCCULENCE IS THE
TRAIT THAT ALLOWS
PLANTS TO SURVIVE
IN HOT, DRY
CLIMATES AND IN
TIMES OF DROUGHT.

"YOU, GOD, are MY GOD, earNestLY i seek YOU; i THirsT For YOU, MY WHOLE BeiNg LONgs For YOU iN a DrY aND ParcHeD LaND WHere THere is No WaTer." Ps 63:1

✾ WHaT Do YOU Do WHeN YoUr FaiTH Feels DrY aND GoD seems Far away?

✾ WHaT PracTiCes MigHT HelP CULTivaTe "SUCCULeNCe" iN YoUr LiFe?

✾ UsiNg THe LiNes oN THe Saguaro cacTUs, WriTe oUT YoUr THoUgHTs...

I AM GOING TO PREPARE A PLACE FOR YOU

JOHN 14:2, MEV

read JOHN 14:1-6.
WHAT are THE Promises Jesus Makes IN
THIS Passage?
Draw a SIMPLE PicTure OF a HOUSE.
THEN, Decorate Your HOUSE WITH THE
Promises From THIS Passage.

SLOWLY READ THROUGH THIS PASSAGE, SONG OF SONGS 2:10-13. NOTICE THE BEAUTIFUL IMAGES USED TO DESCRIBE LOVE. DRAW SIMPLE PICTURES OVER ANY OF THESE WORDS, LIKE RAIN OR FLOWERS. IMMERSE YOURSELF IN GOD'S LOVE.

MY BELOVED SPOKE AND SAID TO ME,

"ARISE MY DARLING,

MY BEAUTIFUL ONE, COME WITH ME.

SEE! THE WINTER IS PAST;

THE RAINS ARE OVER AND GONE.

FLOWERS APPEAR ON THE EARTH;

THE SEASON OF SINGING HAS COME,

THE COOING OF DOVES

IS HEARD IN OUR LAND.

THE FIG TREE FORMS ITS EARLY FRUIT;

THE BLOSSOMING VINES

SPREAD THEIR FRAGRANCE.

ARISE, COME MY DARLING,

MY BEAUTIFUL ONE, COME WITH ME."

The kingdom of heaven is like a merchant looking for fine pearls. When he found one of great value, he went away and sold everything he had and bought it.

Matthew 13:45-46.

12

The merchant sold all he had to gain the "one pearl of great value". How is Jesus the pearl of great value to you? Write about it here...

Picture God as the merchant and YOU as the pearl of great value. God delights in you. He has done everything to "buy" you back. What is your response to Him?

FIND a PICTURe OF YOUR-
SELF AS a BABY. TAPE
iT HeRe. read PSaLM 139:13-16
aND SLOWLY wriTe iT
around YOUR PiCTURe.
WHaT DOeS iT MeaN
TO YOU THaT YOU are
FearFULLY & WONDeRFULLY
MaDe? DO YOU HaVE aNY
DIFFICULTY BELIEViNG
THiS aBOUT YOURSELF?

A Garment of Praise

In Isaiah 61:3, we are encouraged to put on "a garment of praise instead of a spirit of despair". Praise is acknowledging who God is.

Create your own garment of praise. Turn to the back of the book for a list of the names of God. Which names describe the ways you've seen God work in your life? How would you like to experience Him today? Write those on her dress.

 THIS IS THE CHINESE SYMBOL FOR BLESSING. HOW ARE YOU BLESSED? WRITE THEM HERE...

"THERE SHALL BE SHOWERS, SHOWERS OF BLESSING." EZEKIEL 34:26, TLB

Live Care Free Before God; He is Most Careful With You.

I Peter 5:7, MSG

20

WHAT WOULD
IT LOOK LIKE
FOR YOU
TO LIVE
CAREFREE?

HOW HAVE
YOU SEEN
GOD'S CARE
FOR YOU
LATELY?

THORNS

"i was given a thorn in my flesh..."
2 Cor 12:7

read 2 Corinthians 12:7-9.

- WHAT are SOME OF THE "THORNS" YOU HAVE EXPERIENCED, THOSE DIFFICULT PARTS OF YOUR LIFE THAT aren't easily FIXED or CHANGED?

- i've DRAWN a FEW STEMS HERE. aDD YOUR OWN STEMS AND LABEL THEM WITH YOUR THORNS.

- CONSIDER HOW YOUR FAITH HAS grown or CHANGED BECAUSE OF YOUR THORNS. Write aBOUT iT...

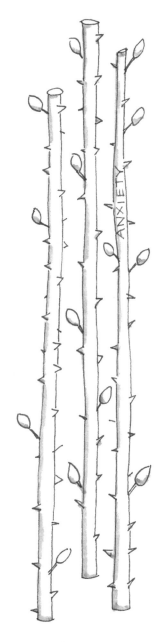

" i have thanked you a thousand times for my roses.
But not once for my thorns... teach me the value of
my thorns." ~ George Matheson

read isaiah 43:1-2. then write it out, inside the letters "you are mine". what promises is God offering you for the hard places in your life?

HAND PRAYERS

TRACE SOMEONE'S HAND HERE. ⇢

THEN, ASK THEM HOW YOU CAN PRAY FOR THEM ... WRITE THOSE NEEDS AROUND THE OUTSIDE OF THEIR TRACED HAND. THEN PUT YOUR HAND OVER THEIR TRACED HAND AND PRAY FOR THOSE NEEDS FOR THEM.

SO DO NOT FEAR FOR I AM WITH YOU; DO NOT BE DISMAYED, FOR I AM YOUR GOD. I WILL STRENGTHEN YOU AND HELP YOU; I WILL UPHOLD YOU WITH MY RIGHTEOUS RIGHT HAND.

ISAIAH 41:10

LOOK AT YOURSELF IN A MIRROR. WHAT TRAITS IN YOURSELF DO YOU STRUGGLE TO ACCEPT— PHYSICALLY, MENTALLY, OR EMOTIONALLY? ON A SEPARATE PIECE OF PAPER, WRITE THOSE DOWN... THEN TEAR IT UP & THROW IT AWAY. NEXT, ASK GOD HOW HE SEES YOU. ASK HIM TO SHOW YOU WHAT HE PARTICULARLY LIKES ABOUT THE WAY HE CREATED YOU. WRITE THESE "WHISPERS OF GOD" IN THE WORD BUBBLES OVER THE MIRROR.

"THIS iS HOW WE KNOW THAT WE BELONG TO THE TRUTH aND HOW WE SET OUR HEARTS AT REST IN HIS PRESENCE: IF OUR HEARTS CONDEMN US, WE KNOW THAT GOD iS GREATER THAN OUR HEARTS, aND HE KNOWS EVERYTHING." I JOHN 3:19-20

WHAT IS ONE THING YOU NEED RIGHT NOW (LIKE JOY OR HOPE OR HEALING)? WRITE THAT ONE

Word over & over & over. Use DiFFeReNT coLors, sizes, all caps, skinny & fat letters... mix it up!

WE NOW HAVE THIS LIGHT SHINING IN OUR HEARTS, BUT WE OURSELVES ARE LIKE FRAGILE CLAY JARS CONTAINING THIS GREAT TREASURE.

2 COR. 4:7, NLT

READ 2 CORINTHIANS 4:6-10. AS YOU LOOK AT THIS PASSAGE AND THESE CRACKED CLAY JARS, CONSIDER:

- HOW HAVE YOU SEEN GOD'S POWER SHINE THROUGH THE WEAK AND BROKEN PLACES IN YOUR LIFE?
- HAS HE USED YOUR BROKEN PLACES TO HELP ANYONE ELSE? OR TO BRING FREEDOM IN YOUR OWN HEART?
- DRAW LINES REPRESENTING RAYS OF LIGHT SHINING THROUGH THE CRACKS IN THE JARS. JOURNAL YOUR THOUGHTS ON THE RAYS OF LIGHT.

TRINITY KNOT

...Glory that you gave me

I have given them the

That they may be one

...as we are one.

John 17:22

This symbol of the Trinity represents the unity between God the Father, Jesus Christ, and the Holy Spirit.

In John 17:22, Jesus expresses his longing for unity among His followers. Slowly read this passage from Philippians 2:1-4, MSG

"If you've gotten anything at all out of following Christ, if his love has made any difference in your life, if being in a community of the Spirit means anything to you, if you have a heart, if you care—then do me a favor: Agree with each other, love each other, be deep-spirited friends. Don't push your way to the front; don't sweet-talk your way to the top. Put yourself aside, and help others get ahead. Don't be obsessed with getting your own advantage. Forget yourselves long enough to lend a helping hand."

· Circle any words that lead us toward unity.

· When it comes to unity among followers of Jesus, what obstacles do you see around you?

· And in your own heart?

Write the word TRUST in big letters on this mug. On the steam, write out verses on trust... Some verses are listed in the back of the book.

· · · · ·

Where do you struggle to trust? Write about it:

"BUT i TRUST iN YOUR UNFAiLING LOVE..." PS. 13:5

HANDS LIKE INCENSE...

write Your Prayers Here~ (Urling up out of Your

"GOD, COME CLOSE. COME QUICKLY! TREAT MY PRAYERS AS SWEET INCENSE OPEN YOUR EARS—IT'S MY VOICE YOU'RE HEARING! RISING, MY RAISED HANDS ARE MY EVENING PRAYERS."

PS 141:2

MSW

Using Fancy Letters and Page with Things that Make

"For You Make Me glad

SIMPLE DRAWINGS, FILL THIS Your HEART GLAD. ♡

BY Your DEEDS, O LorD." PS. 92:4

THINK OF PEOPLE YOU WANT TO DRAW A SIMPLE PICTURE OF THEIR FACE, SYMBOLIZES THEM. THEN, THINK OF & WRITE IT UNDER THEIR FRAME.

Pray for in these little frames, or their initials, or something that a word you'd like to pray for James 5:16 "...pray for each other."

43

WHEN SOMEONE YOU LOVE IS IN A
CAN BE HARD TO EVEN KNOW HOW
THEIR NAME IN BIG BLOCK
THIS PAGE. INSIDE EACH LETTER
SPECIFIC WORDS FOR THEM.

Dark, difficult place, it
to pray for them. Try writing
LETTERS, FILLING
add scripture verses or
fill in with color & designs.

HELP; DO NOT BE DEAF TO MY WEEPING." PS 39:12

YOU KEEP TRACK OF ALL MY SORROWS. YOU HAVE COLLECTED ALL MY TEARS IN YOUR BOTTLE. PS. 56:8, NLT

WHAT MAKES YOU SAD?
THOSE THINGS THAT MAKE US SAD
ARE PRECIOUS TO GOD.
HE NOTICES THEM.
THEY MATTER TO HIM.
WRITE ABOUT YOUR SORROWS
ON THIS BOTTLE...

"Blessed is the man who trusts me, God, sticks with God. The woman who trusts me, God. They're like trees replanted in Eden, putting down roots near the rivers— Never a worry through the hottest of summers, Never dropping a leaf, Serene and calm through droughts, Bearing fresh fruit every season." Jeremiah 17:7-8, MSG

IMAGINE HOW IT MIGHT LOOK
IN YOUR LIFE TO PUT DOWN
"ROOTS NEAR THE RIVERS."
WRITE ABOUT THAT HERE...

ARE YOU EXPERIENCING "THE HOTTEST
OF SUMMERS", A PLACE OF PRESSURE OR
STRUGGLE IN YOUR LIFE?
ON THE RIVER FLOWING UNDER THE
TREE, WRITE A PRAYER IN RESPONSE TO
THE STRUGGLE THAT YOU OR
SOMEONE ELSE IS EXPERIENCING.

WHAT FRUIT DO YOU SEE IN YOUR
LIFE?
WRITE THIS FRUIT ON THE APPLES IN
THE TREE, THANKING GOD FOR IT.

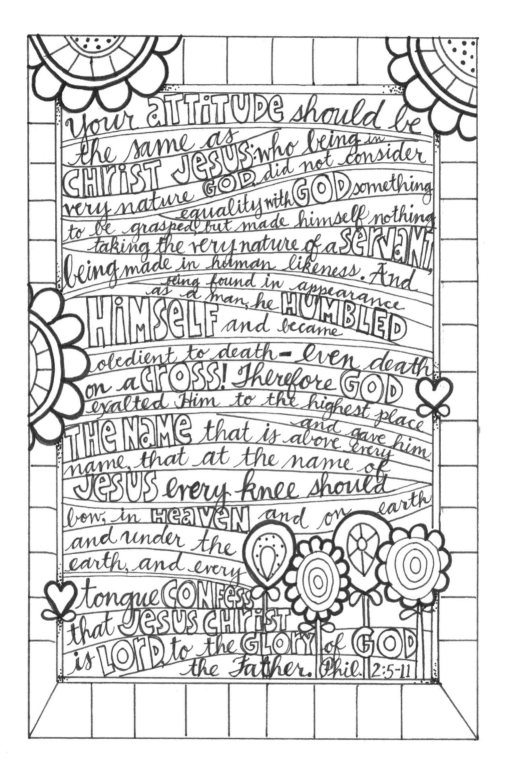

Your attitude should be the same as CHRIST JESUS: who being in very nature GOD, did not consider equality with GOD something to be grasped, but made himself nothing taking the very nature of a SERVANT, being made in human likeness. And being found in appearance as a man, he HUMBLED HIMSELF and became obedient to death — even death on a CROSS! Therefore GOD exalted Him to the highest place and gave him THE NAME that is above every name, that at the name of JESUS every knee should bow, in HEAVEN and on earth and under the earth, and every tongue CONFESS that JESUS CHRIST is LORD, to the GLORY of GOD the Father. Phil. 2:5-11

SPEND SOME TIME MEDITATING ON
PHILIPPIANS 2:5-11 AS YOU ADD COLOR
TO IT.
IS THERE A PLACE IN YOUR LIFE WHERE
YOU SENSE GOD IS ASKING YOU TO BE
A SERVANT?

IS THERE A PLACE WHERE YOU FEEL
HUMBLED, PERHAPS EVEN
UNAPPRECIATED, IN SERVING OR
IN USING YOUR GIFTS?

OFFER THAT TO JESUS AND ASK FOR HIS
HEART TO SERVE IN THOSE PLACES.

"LOVE YOUR as

Draw a simple, little map of your neighborhood. This might be your street or apartment complex or dorm floor. Write your neighbors' names over where they live. As you pray for them, ask the Lord how you might better love your neighbors. Is there something specific he is asking you to do?

Neighbor Yourself."

Mark 12:31

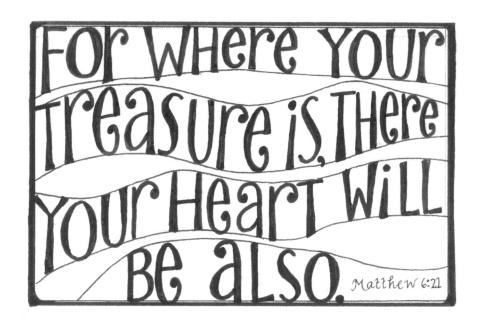

For Where Your Treasure is, There Your Heart Will Be Also. Matthew 6:21

° read LUKE 8:40-56.

° What Thoughts and Words Describe What You Treasure About Jesus in This Passage?

° Fill This Treasure Chest With These Words in Your Own Handwriting or Cut and Glue Words From a Magazine. Add Words Describing How Jesus Has Worked in Your Own Life, Too.

° Let The Words Spill Out and Around The Treasure Chest... Like a Pile of Gold and Precious Jewels.

i Have PLaCeD MY
raiNBOW iN THe
CLouDs. iT is THe
siğn of MY
CoVeNaNT
WiTH YoU
aND WiTH
aLL THe
earTH.
ğenesis 9:13, NLT

rainBows are reminDers oF GoD's goOD promises.

First, coLor Your own rainBow on tHis page. THeN, read THrough some oF GoD's promises To us aT THe Back oF THis BooK, circlinG THe ones THaT grab Your aTTention. Finally, wriTe THe promises THaT got Your aTTention on or unDer Your rainBow.

HOW Beautiful are THE FEET OF THOSE WHO BRinG gOOD NEWS!

romans 10:15

WHO are THE PEOPLE WHO BrOUGHT YOU THE GOOD
NEWS, TELLING YOU ABOUT JESUS? THANK THE LORD
FOr THEM.

are THERE PEOPLE OR PLACES WHERE YOU FEEL CALLED
TO BRING THE GOOD NEWS? WRITE ABOUT IT ON OR
arOUND THESE FEET...

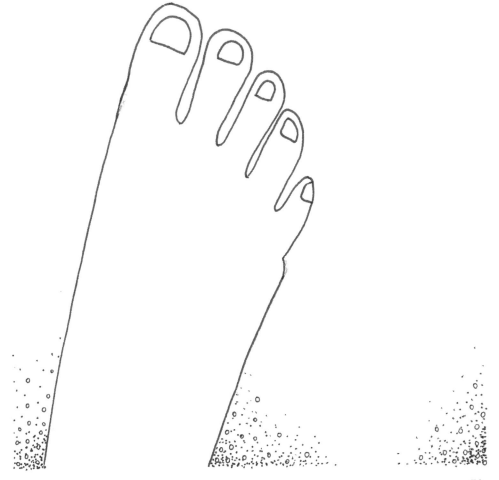

Spray this page with something good smelling... and then add some color...

For we are to God a sweet fragrance of Christ among those who are saved and among those who perish.

2 Corinthians 2:15, MEV

WHere are YoU CaLLeD To Be THe aroMa oF CHriST iN THe WorLD?

WHaT are THe CHaLLeNGes You FaCe as You Do THiS?

WHAT MAKES YOU WORRIED OR AFRAID? MATTHEW 10:30 SAYS THAT GOD CARES ABOUT EVERY BIT OF YOU. HE EVEN KNOWS ALL THE HAIRS ON YOUR HEAD! ON THIS MAN'S HAIR, WRITE OUT THOSE THINGS THAT BURDEN YOU OR WORRY YOU. TRUST THAT GOD CARES AND HEARS YOUR PRAYERS

Draw a cross here ➡

Look up the verses listed around the edge of the page. Which words or phrases grab your heart? Write them out, on or around your cross. Consider why those words spoke to you. Write out a prayer in response...

ROMANS 5:8

GALATIANS 2:20

EPHESIANS 1:7 & 2:13

COLOSSIANS 1:19-20

The Lord deal kindly with you as you have dealt ... with ... me.

Ruth 1:8, ESV

Ask the Lord to help you remember specific acts of kindness that people have shown you. Make a list of them here...

read Joshua 3 & 4, the story of the israelites crossing the Jordan river. remember a time when the Lord provided for you in an unexpected or even a miraculous way. Build your own Memorial of stones on this page. draw twelve stones and label them with the ways God has provided for you.

...THE HAND OF THE LORD iS PowerFUL...

Joshua 4:24

DRIP, DROP, OR DRIZZLE YOUR DRINK ON THIS PAGE... LET IT DRY... WRITE PRAYERS OF CONFESSION OVER IT...

CLEANSE ME WITH HYSSOP AND i WILL BE CLEAN; WASH ME AND i WILL BE WHITER THAN SNOW.   PS. 51:7

ARE THERE PLACES WHERE YOU HANG ONTO BITTER FEELINGS OR FEARS? PLACES WHERE YOU STRUGGLE WITH GREED, JEALOUSY, OR LOOK DOWN ON OTHERS?

IT IS FOR FREEDOM THAT CHRIST HAS SET US FREE. STAND FIRM, THEN, AND DO NOT LET YOURSELVES BE BURDENED AGAIN BY A YOKE OF SLAVERY. GALATIANS 5:1

- HOLDING A GRUDGE IS LIKE PUTTING YOURSELF IN PRISON, MAKING YOU A SLAVE TO PAST PAIN AND HURT. IS THERE SOMEONE YOU ARE STRUGGLING TO FORGIVE? THE ROAD TO FORGIVENESS CAN BE LONG, ESPECIALLY WHEN THE PAIN IS DEEP.

- HERE'S SOMETHING TO TRY... ON THIS HEART, WRITE THAT PERSON'S NAME OR INITIALS. THEN, WRITE A PRAYER OF FORGIVENESS.

- THANK THE LORD THAT EVEN A STRUGGLING ATTEMPT TO FORGIVE IS A STEP TOWARD FREEDOM.

To Forgive is To Set a Prisoner Free...

AND DISCOVER THE PRISONER WAS YOU.

—LEWIS B. SMEDES

FROM THE rising OF THE SUN
THE NAME OF THE

BEFORE YOU go TO SLEEP, ASK THE LORD
JOURNAL YOUR REFLECTIONS TO THESE
  • WHAT are YOU grateful
  • WHAT EMOTIONS DID YOU
 • ASK THE LORD TO HELP YOU UNCOVER
  • IS THERE ANYTHING YOU SENSE YOU
 • FINALLY, COLOR a SUNSET OVER YOUR DAY,

To the Place Where it Sets, Lord is to Be Praised. Ps. 113:3

To help you look back at your day.

Questions in the space above...

For in the day?

Experience during the day?

The roots of these emotions.

Should do in response to your day?

Thanking God for his presence.

Names of God

Abba
Adored
Advocate
All in All
Amen
Ancient of Days
Anointed One
Architect
Author of Our Faith

Beginning
Beloved
Blessed
Bread of Life
Breath
Bridegroom
Bright Morning Star
Branch
Builder

Chief Shepherd
Companion
Comforter
Compassionate
Conqueror
Consuming Fire
Counselor
Crown of Beauty

Dayspring
Defender
Delight
Desire
Door

Emmanuel
Eternal God
Expert
Encourager
Enduring
Everlasting
Exalted
Example

Fairest
Faithful and True

Father of Lights
Firstborn
Forgiving
Fortress
Fountain
Friend

Gardener
Gatherer
Gentle Whisper
Giver
Good Shepherd
Guardian

Hand
Healer
Helper
Hiding Place
Home
Holy One
Hope

I AM
Incomparable
Infinite
Intercessor
Invincible

Jealous
Jesus
Joy
Judge
Just

Keeper
Key
King of Glory
King of Kings
Kinsman

Life
Lion of Judah
Living Water
Light of the World
Lord
Loving Kindness

Majesty
Maker
Man of Sorrows
Manna
Merciful
Mighty God
Morning Star

Nazarene
New
Needed
Nurturer

Only Begotten Son
Omega
Our Passover Lamb
Our Peace
Overcomer

Paraclete
Pearl Merchant
Physician
Potter
Protector
Provider
Precious

Quickening Spirit
Queller of Storms

Radiance
Ransom
Redeemer
Refresher
Refuge
Resurrection
Road
Rock
Ruler

Sacrifice
Salvation
Sanctuary
Savior
Seed
Servant

Shade
Shepherd
Shield
Son of God
Son of Man
Song
Source
Sovereign
Sower
Spirit
Star
Stronghold
Strong Tower
Sun

Teacher
Temple
Tender
Transformer
Trustworthy
Truth

Unchangeable
Understanding
Undefeated
Unfailing
Upright One
Unlimited

Very Great Reward
Victory
Vine

Way
Wine
Wise
Witness
Wonderful
Word

Yahweh
Yearning

Zeal

Verses on Trust

Those who know your name trust in you, for you, LORD, have never forsaken those who seek you.—Psalm 9:10

But I trust in your unfailing love. I will rejoice because you have rescued me.—Psalm 13:5 NLT

The Lord is my strength and shield. I trust him with all my heart. He helps me, and my heart is filled with joy. I burst out in songs of thanksgiving.—Psalm 28:7 NLT

But I am like an olive tree flourishing in the house of God; I trust in God's unfailing love forever and ever.—Psalm 52:8

Praise the LORD. Blessed are those who fear the LORD, who find great delight in his commands. . . . They will have no fear of bad news; their hearts are steadfast, trusting in the LORD.—Psalm 112:1, 7

Trust GOD from the bottom of your heart; don't try to figure out everything on your own. Listen for GOD's voice in everything you do, everywhere you go; he's the one who will keep you on track.—Proverbs 3:5–6 MSG

Surely God is my salvation; I will trust and not be afraid. The LORD, the LORD himself, is my strength and my defense; he has become my salvation.—Isaiah 12:2

. . . In repentance and rest is your salvation, in quietness and trust is your strength . . .—Isaiah 30:15

But those who trust in the Lord will find new strength. They will soar high on wings like eagles. They will run and not grow weary. They will walk and not faint.—Isaiah 40:31 NLT

The LORD is good, a strong refuge when trouble comes. He is close to those who trust in him.—Nahum 1:7 NLT

Put your trust in the light while there is still time; then you will become children of the light . . .—John 12:36 NLT

Do not let your hearts be troubled. You believe in God; believe also in me.—John 14:1

May the God of hope fill you with all joy and peace as you trust in him, so that you may overflow with hope by the power of the Holy Spirit.—Romans 15:13

We are confident of all this because of our great trust in God through Christ. It is not that we think we are qualified to do anything on our own. Our qualification comes from God.—2 Corinthians 3:4–5 NLT

When we trust in him, we're free to say whatever needs to be said, bold to go wherever we need to go.—Ephesians 3:12 MSG

I pray that from his glorious, unlimited resources he will empower you with inner strength through his Spirit. Then Christ will make his home in your hearts as you trust in him. Your roots will grow down into God's love and keep you strong.—Ephesians 3:16–17 NLT

And since we have a great High Priest who rules over God's house, let us go right into the presence of God with sincere hearts fully trusting him. For our guilty consciences have been sprinkled with Christ's blood to make us clean, and our bodies have been washed with pure water.—Hebrews 10:21–22 NLT

So do not throw away this confident trust in the Lord. Remember the great reward it brings you!—Hebrews 10:35 NLT

Promises From God

God is our refuge and strength, an ever-present help in trouble.—Psalm 46:1

For his unfailing love toward those who fear him is as great as the height of the heavens above the earth. He has removed our sins as far from us as the east is from the west.—Psalm 103:11–12 NLT

Don't be afraid, for I am with you. Don't be discouraged, for I am your God. I will strengthen you and help you. I will hold you up with my victorious right hand.—Isaiah 41:10 NLT

I will give you a new heart and put a new spirit in you; I will remove from you your heart of stone and give you a heart of flesh.—Ezekiel 36:26

That is why I tell you not to worry about everyday life—whether you have enough food and drink, or enough clothes to wear. Isn't life more than food, and your body more than clothing? Look at the birds. They don't plant or harvest or store food in barns, for your heavenly Father feeds them. And aren't you far more valuable to him than they are?—Matthew 6:25–26 NLT

Come to me, all you who are weary and burdened, and I will give you rest. Take my yoke upon you and learn from me, for I am gentle and humble in heart, and you will find rest for your souls. For my yoke is easy and my burden is light.—Matthew 11:28–30

I am the vine; you are the branches. If you remain in me and I in you, you will bear much fruit; apart from me you can do nothing.—John 15:5

Now all glory to God, who is able, through his mighty power at work within us, to accomplish infinitely more than we might ask or think.—Ephesians 3:20 NLT

And we know that in all things God works for the good of those who love him, who have been called according to his purpose.—Romans 8:28

For I am convinced that neither death nor life, neither angels nor demons, neither the present nor the future, nor any powers, neither height nor depth, nor anything else in all creation, will be able to separate us from the love of God that is in Christ Jesus our Lord.—Romans 8:38–39

The temptations in your life are no different from what others experience. And God is faithful. He will not allow the temptation to be more than you can stand. When you are tempted, he will show you a way out so that you can endure.—1 Corinthians 10:13 NLT

So let's not get tired of doing what is good. At just the right time we will reap a harvest of blessing if we don't give up.—Galatians 6:9 NLT

Whatever I have, wherever I am, I can make it through anything in the One who makes me who I am.—Philippians 4:13 MSG

And my God will meet all your needs according to the riches of his glory in Christ Jesus.—Philippians 4:19

If you need wisdom, ask our generous God, and he will give it to you. He will not rebuke you for asking.—James 1:5 NLT

Cast all your anxiety on him because he cares for you.—1 Peter 5:7

He will wipe every tear from their eyes. There will be no more death or mourning or crying or pain, for the old order of things has passed away.—Revelation 21:4

Acknowledgments

Thanks to dear friends in Denver, Phoenix, and other places for your feedback (you make great guinea pigs!) and for leaning into this process with me. The Lord has used you all to love me well. Kaley, thanks for letting me use your house idea. And I am appreciative for the clever Young Life people who came up with the hand prayers (whomever they may be). Many thanks to my agent, Andrew Wolgemuth, for helping to develop this concept, and for all the encouragement along the way. And thank you to Andy McGuire and the folks at Bethany House for your beautiful collaborative efforts and for taking a chance on a different sort of project.

I am grateful for my mom, who encouraged artsy fun in our home, and my brothers, who were game for trying something new—if we could do it together. Thank you to all my in-laws, for your interest and loving encouragement. Thank you to our kids (John 3, Anna, Austin, Grace, Scott, and of course, little Margaret) for sharing your editing skills and cheering me on toward the finish line. And bless my dear husband, John. Words don't do justice to the lovely way you love and serve me, and our family. You are God's good gift to me.

Connecting with Jesus through creativity has been a significant part of **Gayla Irwin's** spiritual journey. She is blessed by her family (especially her baby granddaughter), the beauty of the mountains, books, new markers, and shoes. Gayla and her husband, John, serve together as executive directors of a retreat house in Denver, Colorado. She has been long involved with Young Life, most recently in the area of leadership development. Trained as a spiritual director and ministry coach, she enjoys creating experiences that help others nurture intimacy with Jesus. To learn more visit gaylairwin.com.